AAT

Applied Management Accounting

Pocket Notes

These Pocket Notes support study for the following AAT qualifications:

AAT Diploma in Professional Accounting – Level 4

AAT Diploma in Business Skills – Level 4

AAT Diploma in Professional Accounting at SCQF Level 8

British library cataloguing-in-publication data

A catalogue record for this book is available from the British Library.

Published by:
Kaplan Publishing UK
Unit 2 The Business Centre
Molly Millars Lane
Wokingham
Berkshire
RG41 2QZ

ISBN 978-1-83996-080-2

© Kaplan Financial Limited, 2021

Printed and bound in Great Britain.

The text in this material and any others made available by any Kaplan Group company does not amount to advice on a particular matter and should not be taken as such. No reliance should be placed on the content as the basis for any investment or other decision or in connection with any advice given to third parties. Please consult your appropriate professional adviser as necessary. Kaplan Publishing Limited and all other Kaplan group companies expressly disclaim all liability to any person in respect of any losses or other claims, whether direct, indirect, incidental, consequential or otherwise arising in relation to the use of such materials.

CONTENTS

Preface

These Pocket Notes contain the key things that you need to know for the assessment, presented in a unique visual way that makes revision easy and effective.

Written by experienced lecturers and authors, these Pocket Notes break down content into manageable chunks to maximise your concentration.

Quality and accuracy are of the utmost importance to us so if you spot an error in any of our products, please send an email to mykaplanreporting@kaplan.com with full details, or follow the link to the feedback form in MyKaplan.

Our Quality Co-ordinator will work with our technical team to verify the error and take action to ensure it is corrected in future editions.

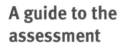

A guide to the assessment

The assessment

AMAC is one of the management accounting units studied on the professional diploma in accounting.

Examination

Applied Management Accounting is assessed by mean of a computer based assessment. The CBA will last for 3 hours.

In any one assessment, students may not be assessed on all content, or on the full depth or breadth of a piece of content. The content assessed may change over time to ensure validity of assessment, but all assessment criteria will be tested over time.

Learning outcomes & weighting

1. Understand and implement the organisational planning process   25%

2. Use internal processes to enhance operational control   30%

3. Use techniques to aid short-term and long-term decision making   25%

4. Analyse and report on business performance   20%

Total   100%

Pass mark

To pass a unit assessment, students need to achieve a mark of 70% or more.

This unit contributes 30% of the total amount required for the Professional Diploma in Accounting qualification.

1

Activity Based Costing

- MC and TAC – summary.
- Activity Based Costing.

MC and TAC – summary

Marginal costing (MC)

In marginal costing, units of inventory are valued incorporating only variable production costs.

- More consistent with short term decision making techniques as most focus on contribution.
- Can also be simpler as fixed costs do not have to be apportioned.
- Cannot boost profit simply by making more units (unlike TAC).

Total absorption costing

In absorption costing, inventories are valued by incorporating all production costs, both fixed and variable.

- Suitable for financial reporting.
- Suitable for 'full cost plus' pricing, ensuring that all costs are covered.
- Profit fluctuates less when faced with seasonal trade.

Overhead absorption is achieved by means of a predetermined Overhead Absorption Rate (OAR).

Chapter 1

Activity Based Costing (ABC)

Step 1 Identify major activities.

Step 2 Identify appropriate cost drivers.

Step 3 Collect costs into pools based upon the activities (note: this is usually done for you in a question/task).

Step 4 Charge costs to units of production based on cost driver rate.

$$\text{Cost driver rate} = \frac{\text{Cost pool}}{\text{Level of cost driver}}$$

Examples of cost drivers

- Machine costs could be charged using machine hours.
- Quality control costs could be charged using number of inspections.
- Set-up costs could be charged using number of set-ups.

Implications of switching to ABC

- Pricing can be based on more realistic cost data.
- Sales strategy can be more soundly based.
- Decision making can be improved.
- Performance management can be improved.

Benefits and Limitations of ABC

Benefits	Limitations
1. Provides more accurate product line costings.	1. Little evidence to date that ABC improves corporate profitability.
2. Is flexible enough to analyse costs by cost objects other than products, such as processes, areas of managerial responsibility and customers.	2. ABC information is historic and internally orientated and therefore lacks direct relevance for future strategic decisions.
3. Provides meaningful financial (periodic cost driver rates) and non-financial (periodic cost driver volume) measures.	3. Practical problems such as cost driver selection.
4. Aids identification and understanding of cost behaviour and thus has the potential to improve cost estimation.	
5. Provides a more logical, acceptable and comprehensible basis for costing work.	

Target costing and life cycle costing

- Lifecycle costing.
- Non discounting.
- Target costing.

Lifecycle costing

All products go through lifecycles

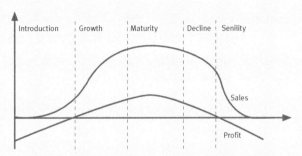

As shown by the difference between the revenue and cost curves, the pattern of costs over the lifecycle does not match that of revenue.

In particular, there will be high development costs during the introduction stage.

Traditional financial accounting has the following problems in this respect:

*   It will look at the profit in a particular year, rather than assessing profitability over the whole lifecycle.

*   Research costs are often written off in the year in which they are incurred rather than matching against (later) revenue.

Non discounting

The non-discounting approach simply adds up all the expected costs associated with the product in question across its entire life, regardless of the time period it is incurred in.

Then it divides it by the total number of units expected to be made and sold over the products entire life.

$$\text{Life cycle costs per unit} = \frac{\text{total costs over its entire life}}{\text{Total number of units}}$$

Interpretation

Many companies find that up to 90% of the product's life-cycle costs are determined by decisions made in the development and launch stages. Focussing on costs after the product has entered production results in only a small proportion of life-cycle costs being manageable.

Life-cycle costing reinforces the importance of tight control over locked-in costs, such as R&D in the development stage.

Discounting

It is also possible to work out the life cycle cost of a project using discounting techniques, the general approach to discounting will be recapped in chapter 13.

Target costing

Many firms operate a 'cost-plus' pricing system, where the selling price of a product is calculated by adding a mark-up to the production cost.

Target costing is the reverse of this process:

1   The firm estimates the likely product price by looking at market conditions, competition, etc.

2   A target mark-up % is deducted from the price to give a target cost.

3   Production then sees if it can produce the product at the cost required.

Example

R plc makes fridges. The current cost per unit is £100 and R sells them for £200, a mark-up of 100%. Due to increased competition, R feels that a selling price of £160 would be more competitive.

Assuming the mark up of 100% is still required, calculate the target cost.

Solution

Target price = £160

Target cost = 160 x 100/200 = £80

The production department needs to try to save £20 per unit on cost.

3

Limiting factor analysis

- Contribution.
- Limiting factors.

Contribution

Contribution is defined as the difference between the selling price and the variable cost of producing and selling the item. This is in contrast to profit per unit, which is the difference between the selling price and the total absorption cost of producing and selling that item, which includes an element of fixed cost.

It is called contribution since it tells us how much each product contributes towards paying for the fixed costs of the business.

Limiting factors

Definition

Key factor analysis is a technique used when we have one resource that is in scarce supply and we can make more than one type of product using that resource. Key factor analysis determines how to use this resource in such a way that profits are maximised.

$$\frac{\text{Contribution per unit}}{\text{Number of units of scarce resource needed}}$$

Approach to key factor analysis

(1) Determine the limiting factor or key factor that is in scarce supply

(2) Calculate the contribution per unit generated by each product

(3) Calculate the contribution per unit of scarce resource for each product

(4) Select the product with the highest contribution per unit of scarce resource and make this first

Example

Basic key factor analysis

Bill makes two products as set out below:

	R	S
	£	£
Selling price	120	50
Material @ £10 per kg	(70)	(25)
	50	25

Bill can sell all the goods he can make, but next year he will be able to purchase only 2,400 kg of material – how should he use this to maximise profits?

	R	S
Contribution per unit	£50	£25
Materials per unit	(£70/£10) 7kg	(£25/£10) 2.5 kg
Contribution per kg	£7.14	£10
Rank	2	1

As S has the higher contribution per unit of scarce resource, Bill should make S.

> Profits are maximised when contribution is maximised

Key factor analysis with demand constraints

Example

Blake Ltd is subject to a restriction of £6,000 worth of labour hours in one month, which are used to make three products.

	A	B	C
	£	£	£
Selling price	80	20	45
Labour cost	(24)	(6)	(15)
Other variable costs	(20)	(8)	(12)
Contribution	36	6	18

Maximum demand levels in any one month are expected to be 200 units for products A and B and 600 units for C.

Rank products

	A	B	C
Contribution per unit	£36	£6	£18
Labour per unit (£)	£24	£6	£15
Contribution per £ of labour	£1.50	£1.00	£1.20
Rank	1	3	2

Optimal production plan

	Units	Labour £	Contribution £
1 Product A (up to maximum 200)	200	4,800	7,200
2 Product C (£1,200 ÷ £15)	80	1,200 (bal)	1,440
3 Product B	–	–	–
		£6,000	£8,640

If a business makes more than one product and does not have enough resources to make all it can sell of all products, it must decide which one(s) to produce in full and which to produce in part. This is done based on **contribution per unit of limiting factor**.

Example

A business makes two products X and Y using the same materials, labour and machine capacity. It keeps no inventory of finished goods. The sales price, sales demand and standard cost of each unit, and current availability of resources, are set out as follows:

Table 1	Product X	Product Y	Current availability
Sales demand in months (units)	1,500	3,000	
	£	£	
Selling price per unit	33.00	63.00	
Materials: 0.75kg / 2kg at £3 per kg	2.25	6.00	7,200 kg
Labour: 1.25hrs / 2.5hrs at £12 per hour	15.00	30.00	9,000 hours
Machine time 0.5hrs / 1 hr at £15 per hour	7.50	15.00	4,000 hours
Contribution per unit	8.25	12.00	

After identifying labour as the limiting factor, the completed production budget is provided as follows:

Table 2: Production budget usage for sales demand	Product X	Product Y	Total required
Materials (kg)	1,125	6,000	7,125
Labour (hours)	1,875	7,500	9,375
Machine time (hours)	750	3,000	3,750
Contribution per unit of limiting factor (labour) (£)	6.60	4.80	
Production (units)	1,500	2,850	

Production of X uses 1,500 x 1,875 hours

Remaining hours available = 9,000 - 1,875 = 7,125

Production of Y: 7,125/2.5 = 2,850 units

4

Linear programming

- Linear programming.

Linear programming

Linear programming is used to establish an optimum product mix when there are two or more resource constraints. This mix will achieve a certain (given) objective. The objective is usually to maximise contribution, but on occasion it is to maximise costs.

1 Define variables

   e.g. "Let x = the number of tables made each month".

2 Define the objective.

   e.g. "Maximise contribution, C = 3x + 5y".

3 Set out constraints

   Non-negativity "x ≥ 0, y ≥ 0"

   Others – e.g. "5x + 2y ≤ 20".

4 Draw graph showing constraints and identify the feasible region.

   • Get end-points of constraint lines – e.g. 5x + 2y = 20 has end points (4,0) , (0,10).

   • Decide on scale and draw lines using end-points.

   • Feasible region is below a line if constraint is "≤" and above the line if "≥".

5 Solve the optimal production plan – draw an example iso-contribution line by making up a suitable value of C. Move this out away from the origin to identify the optimal point – it should be the last point you get to that is still feasible.

   Note: if the objective is to minimise costs, then an iso-cost line will need to be moved towards the origin.

   Determine the optimal solution exactly by solving simultaneously the equations of the two lines that cross at the optimal point identified on the graph.

   • Scale up one or both equations until they have the same number of "y" (or "x").

Chapter 4

- Look at difference between the two (adjusted) equations and solve for "x" (or "y", as appropriate).

- Substitute the value of "x" (or "y") back into either of the two critical constraint equations and solve for "y" (or "x").

6   Answer the question!

- Calculate the maximum contribution / minimum cost.

- Write a recommendation to management.

Note: step 5 can be replaced with the following:

Determine the coordinates of each of the corners of the feasible region using simultaneous equations.

For each of the corners calculate the contribution and select the corner with the highest contribution.

Simultaneous equation example:

$6X + 8Y = 36$ (i)

$10X + 4Y = 32$ (ii)

Multiply (ii) by 2 to give:

$20X + 8Y = 64$ we'll call this (iii)

Subtract (i) from (iii):

$(20X - 6X) + (8Y - 8Y) = (64 - 36)$

$14X + 0 = 28$

$X = 28 \div 14 = 2$

Substitute $X = 2$ into (i) to find Y

$(6 \times 2) + 8Y = 36$

$12 + 8Y = 36$

$8Y = 36 - 12 = 24$

$Y = 24 \div 8 = 3$

Assumptions

Assumption	Reality
• A single quantifiable objective exists e.g. to maximise contribution.	• Multiple objectives (e.g. risk, return).
	• Learning effects.
• Each product always uses the same quantity of the scarce resources per unit.	• The selling price may have to be lowered to sell more.
• The contribution per unit is constant.	• Discounts as the quantity of materials needed increases.
	• Economies of scale.
	• Customers may expect to buy both products together.
• Products are independent – e.g. sell A not B.	• The products may be manufactured jointly together.
• The scenario is short term.	• In the long term constraints can be changed and fixed costs should be included.

5

Short term decision making

- Relevant costing.
- Other decision making techniques.
- Make v buy decisions.
- Shut down decisions.
- Joint products – the further processing decision.

Relevant costing

Relevant costs and revenues are those costs and revenues that change as a direct result of a decision taken.

They have the following characteristics:

- Future – we ignore costs the have already been incurred
- Incremental – we therefore ignore most fixed costs (unless they change because of the decision) and all committed costs
- Cash flows – we ignore accounting adjustments such as depreciation.

Other terms used in decision making:

Sunk costs	Expenditure that has already been incurred and therefore will not be relevant to the investment decision.
Committed costs	Expenditure that will be incurred in the future, but as a result of decisions taken in the past that cannot now be changed.
	These are not treated as relevant costs for decision making.
Opportunity cost	The value of the benefit sacrificed when one course of action is chosen, in preference to an alternative. The opportunity cost is represented by the forgone potential benefit from the best rejected course of action.
	These costs usually become relevant when resources are scarce.

Other decision making techniques

Make or buy / outsourcing	If the variable cost of producing the product internally is less than the cost of purchasing the product from the external market and the fixed costs are unavoidable, then the company should produce internally.
Shutdown	If the product/department is generating a positive contribution and the fixed costs are unavoidable, then it should not be shut down.
Mechanisation	If the cost of using machinery to complete a process is cheaper than a manual labour process then the process should be mechanised.

Other considerations / risks:

- Impact on employee morale
- Quality
- Competitor reaction

- Alternative use of resources
- Reliability
- Customer reaction

Make v buy decisions

Decision

- Look at future incremental cash flows.

- Watch out for opportunity costs – especially whether or not spare capacity exists and alternative uses for capacity.

Practical factors

- Can the external supplier deliver sufficient quantity and quality as and when needed?

- Control of quality and delivery.

- The external supplier may possess specialist skills.

- Social factors, e.g. outsourcing may result in redundancies.

- Legal factors, e.g. outsourcing may impact contractual obligations.

- Alternative use of resources.

- Customer perception – customers may value products being made in-house.

- Confidentiality – buying in gives other companies some information about how the product is made.

Shut down decisions

Decision

- Look at future incremental cash flows.
- Apportioned overheads not relevant – only include specific incremental costs.
- Closure costs – e.g. penalties, redundancies.
- Reorganisation costs.
- Alternative uses for resources – e.g. make an alternative product?

Practical factors

- There may be additional costs, e.g. reorganisation costs which are unquantifiable at present.
- Impact on customers – e.g. expect a wide portfolio of products.
- Impact on other products – e.g. may be a loss leader.

Joint products – the further processing decision

Decision

- Look at future incremental cash flows: sell at split off v process further and then sell.
- Pre-separation ("joint") costs not relevant – only include post split-off aspects.

6

Calculating forecasts

- Index numbers.
- Time series analysis.
- Linear regression.
- Expected values.

Index numbers

Calculating an index

Index numbers are used to show changes in values from one period to another. A particular date is chosen as the base period. The index for the base period is always 100.0.

Example

Year	Price of loaf of bread (in pence)	Index	
20X0	51		100.0
20X1	56	56/51 x 100 =	109.8
20X2	59	59/51 x 100 =	115.7
20X3	62	62/51 x 100 =	121.6

Notice how the index is calculated: divide the value in the year you are looking at by the value in the base year, then multiply by 100.

Rebasing

This is when we change the base period. In the example above, assume we change the base period to 20X2.

Year	Original index	Rebased index			Check		
20X0	100.0	100/115.7 x 100	=	86.4	51/59 x 100	=	86.4
20X1	109.8	109.8/115.7 x 100	=	94.9	56/59 x 100	=	94.9
20X2	115.7	100.0			59/59 x 100	=	100.0
20X3	121.6	121.6/115.7 x 100	=	105.1	62/59 x 100	=	105.1

Time series analysis

- method of forecasting sales quantities for budgeting purposes
- isolate trend using moving averages
- calculate seasonal variations
- forecast future sales levels with time series
- moving averages.

By using moving averages, the effect of any seasonal variation in a time series can be eliminated to show the basic trend. This elimination process will only work if the moving average is calculated over the correct number of values (being the number of values in one complete cycle).

- The additive model.

Actual data (time series) = T + S + C + R

T = trend; S = seasonal variation; C = cyclical variation; R = random variation. For AMAC we only use trend and seasonal variation.

Example

You are given the quarterly sales figures and seasonal variations for the last year:

	Actual sales	Seasonal variation
	£000	£000
Quarter 1	100	−20
Quarter 2	140	+10
Quarter 3	140	0
Quarter 4	90	−60

Calculate the trend using the additive model: A = T + S
(or rearranged: T = A − S)

Solution

	Actual sales	Seasonal variation	Trend
	£000	£000	£000
Q 1	100	−20	120
Q 2	140	+10	130
Q 3	140	0	140
Q 4	90	-60	150

+10
+10
+10

The quarterly trend is an increase in sales of £10,000.

Linear regression

Regression involves using historical data to find the line of best fit ($y = a + bx$) between 2 variables (one dependent on the other), and uses this to predict future values.

b	is the gradient or slope – the change in y when x increases by one unit.	a	is the intercept on the y axis when x equals zero.

Disadvantages of linear regression

- It assumes a linear relationship.
- Based on historic information.
- Ignores other (external) factors.

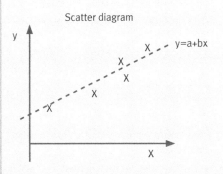

Scatter diagram

Expected values

- EV = $\sum$ outcome × probability.
- Make decision based on best EV.

Advantages	Disadvantages
• Calculations are relatively simple.	• The probabilities used are usually very subjective.
• Takes risk into account.	• The EV is the average payoff if the project is repeated many times. Not useful for one-off decisions.
• Information is reduced to a single number resulting in easier decisions.	• The EV gives no indication of the dispersion of possible outcomes about the expected value. The dispersion gives information about the risk.
	• The EV may not correspond to any of the actual outcomes.

chapter

7

Introduction to budgeting

- Planning, budgeting and forecasting.
- The purpose of budgets.
- Preparing budgets.
- Responsibility accounting.
- Participation in budget setting.
- Sources of information.
- Basic methods of budgeting

Planning, budgeting and forecasting

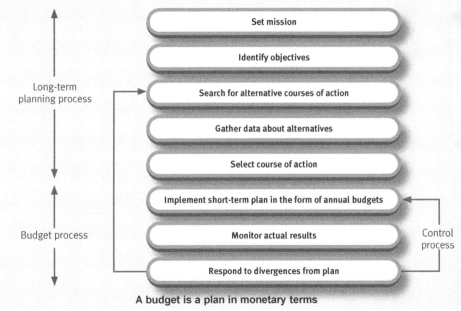

A budget is a plan in monetary terms

The purpose of budgets

A budget is a quantitative expression of a plan of action prepared in advance of the period to which it relates.

- Budgets set out the costs and revenues that are expected to be incurred or earned in future periods.

Co-ordinating activities   Planning for the future

Communication of targets

Controlling costs

BUDGETS

Motivation

Performance evaluation

Authorisation of expenditure

Preparing budgets

Stages in budget preparation

> Define long term objectives of the business

↓

> Form budget committee to communicate budget policy, set and approve budgets.
>
> Budget committee often includes:
>
> - Chief executive
> - Budget officer (management accountant)
> - Departmental or functional heads

↓

> Produce budget manual.
>
> - Instructions on preparing and using budgets
> - Details of responsibilities – including organisation chart and list of budget holders

↓

> Identify principal budget factor – the limiting factor which limits the activity of the organisation.
>
> - Usually sales but could be a scarce resource

↓

> Produce budget for principal budget factor

↓

> Produce and approve other budgets based on budget for limiting factor

↓

> Review actual results and compare with budget to calculate variances

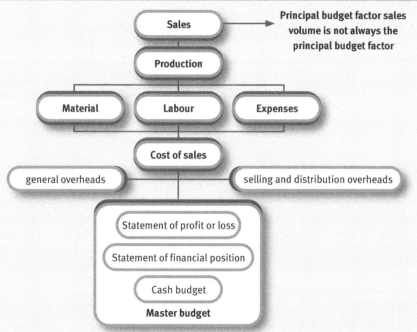

Responsibility accounting

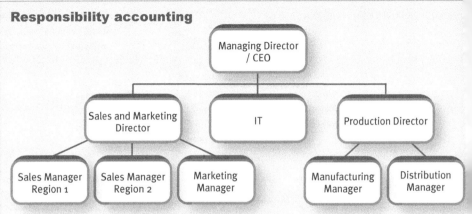

The entire organisation should be divided into various responsibility centres. Each responsibility centre is held by a manager or head of the centre, who has been assigned the responsibility for its budget.

Each responsibility centre should be classified into one of the following categories:

1. Revenue and expense centres;

2. Profit centres;

3. Investment centres.

Participation in budget setting

Target setting and motivation

Targets will assist motivation and appraisal if they are at the right level.

- Too hard and people give up.
- Too easy and people won't try hard enough.

An ideal target should be slightly above the anticipated performance level.

Targets should be:

- Communicated in advance.
- Dependent on factors controllable by the individual.
- Based on quantifiable factors.
- Linked to appropriate rewards and penalties.
- Chosen carefully to ensure goal congruence.
- Challenging but achievable.

Participation is generally agreed to help.

Participation

Top-down budgeting (non-participative)

A budget which is set without allowing the ultimate budget holder to have the opportunity to participate in the budgeting process.

Bottom-up budgeting (participative)

A system of budgeting in which budget holders have the opportunity to participate in setting their own budgets.

Advantages of participative budgets	Disadvantages of participative budgets
1. Increased motivation.	1. Senior managers may resent loss of control.
2. Should contain better information, especially in a fast-moving or diverse business.	2. Bad decisions from inexperienced managers.
3. Increases managers' understanding and commitment.	3. Budgets may not be in line with corporate objectives.
4. Better communication.	4. Budget preparation is slower and disputes can arise.
5. Senior managers can concentrate on strategy.	5. Figures may be subject to bias if junior managers either try to impress or set easily achievable targets (budgetary slack).
	6. Certain environments may preclude participation, e.g. sales manager may be faced with long-term contracts already agreed.

Sources of information

Internal sources of information

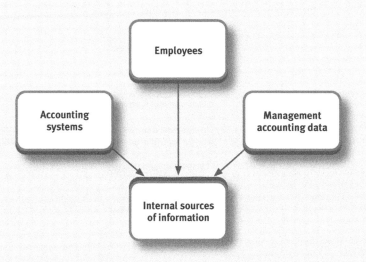

External sources of information

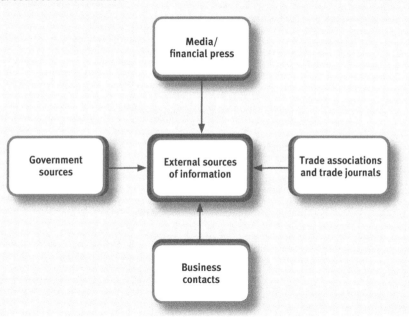

Basic methods of budgeting

Incremental (historic)	Zero-based budgeting	Priority-based budgeting	Activity-based budgeting
Starts with previous period's budget or actual results and adds (or subtracts) an incremental amount to cover inflation and other known changes.	Requires cost element to be specifically justified, as though the activities to which the budget relates were being undertaken for the first time.	A competitively ranked listing of high to low priority discrete bids for "decision packages." • All activities are re-evaluated each time a budget is set. • Does not require a zero assumption.	Preparing budgets using overhead costs from activity based costing methodology

Rolling budges

Continuously updated

Incremental (historic)	Zero-based budgeting
Suitable for stable businesses, where costs are not expected to change significantly.	Without approval, the budget allowance is zero.
There should be good cost control and limited discretionary costs.	Suitable for allocating resources in areas were spend is discretionary.

8

Budgeting Process

- Budget preparation.
- Functional budgets.
- Cash budgeting.

Budget preparation

Stages in budget preparation

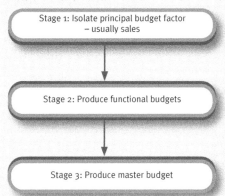

Stage 1: Isolate principal budget factor
– usually sales

Stage 2: Produce functional budgets

Stage 3: Produce master budget

Functional budgets

Typical steps

Sales forecast

Adjust for inventory of finished goods

Production budget

Materials usage budget

Overhead budget

Labour utilisation budget

Adjust for inventory of materials

Materials purchases inventory budget

Labour cost budget

Typical calculations

- **Budgeted production = Forecast sales + closing inventory of finished goods – opening inventory of finished goods.**

- **Materials Usage = Usage per unit x units produced.**

- **Materials purchases budget = forecast materials usage + closing inventory of materials – opening inventory of materials.**

- If dealing with more than one product, keep them separate (side by side in workings) except when producing the materials purchases budget. Here you will need to aggregate the material requirements for both products together.

For the materials budget you'll need to know:

- the amount used per unit of finished goods
- opening and closing inventory of materials
- any allowance for wastage of materials
- the purchase price per unit of material.

Total materials purchases and costs in a month (assuming 5% wastage) is shown here.

	Units (litres, kg, metres)	
Materials for production	M	95%
Add: Wastage M x (5/95)	X	5%
Materials usage	X	100%
Add: closing inventory	X	
Less: opening inventory	-X	
Purchases	Q	
Purchase price per unit	$P	
Purchase cost Q x $P	$X	

Complications

Opening and closing inventories

A business needs a production budget. A production budget plans how much output should be produced for a period.

To prepare this, it needs a format for the budget document to be filled in by the Accounting Technician. It also needs information about opening and closing inventory levels from the Production Director.

Production budget	Quantity in units	
	January	February
Opening inventory at the start of the month	4000	3500
Production in month	5500	4800
Sub-total	**9500**	**8300**
Sales in month (units)	6000	4400
Closing inventory at the end of the month	3500	3900

Production required for the month = Sales quantity + Closing inventory quantity - Opening Inventory quantity.

For each month, closing inventory is usually a percentage of the next month's sales. It may also be expressed as the number of days' sales to be held.

Complications

Wastage of completed units

The production budget also includes the rejection of finished goods that are not fit for sale.

Example

In September a firm plans to sell 161 units. It has 20 units of opening inventory, wants 30 units of closing inventory and typically finds that 5% of units made fail quality control.

How many units of production should be planned?

Solution

Sales	161
Less: opening inventory	(20)
Plus: closing inventory	30
Production of good units needed	171
Production budget = 171/0.95	**180**

Wastage of raw materials

This is very similar to wastage of completed units except that the adjustment is made to materials usage.

Example

Continuing the above example, each unit of output uses 2kg of material. 40% of materials input into the production process are wasted. Determine the materials usage budget?

Solution

Production budget	180 units
Material content of production output (180 x 2)	360kg
Materials usage budget (i.e. input) = 360/0.6	600kg

For the **labour budget** you'll need to know:

- the hours spent used per unit
- any allowance for inefficiency of labour
- the number of basic hours available
- the rate of pay per basic hour
- the rate of pay for overtime.

Total labour hours and cost in a month (assuming 5% inefficiency) is shown here.

	Hours/$	
Labour for production	L	95%
Add: Inefficiency L x 5 /95	X	5%
Labour hours needed	H	100%
Basic hours available	B	
Overtime hours needed	0	H-B
Basic rate	$R	
Basic hours cost B x $R	$X	
Overtime rate	$P	
Overtime hours cost O x $P	$X	

Wages

The two complications that occur with wages are overtime and minimum guaranteed wages. The key is to compare the labour utilisation with the limits for overtime and guarantees.

Example

Z plc pays its workforce \$8/hr with overtime at time-and-a-half when an individual works more than 50 hours in a week. There is also an agreement that the weekly wage should not fall below \$240 (i.e. 30 hours' worth).

In October the following work was planned for a particular employee. Calculate the wages for the month.

Week	1	2	3	4
Hours	35	40	25	55

Solution

Week	1	2	3	4
Hours	35	40	25	55
Hours paid @\$8	35	40	30	50
Hours paid @\$12	0	0	0	5
Total wages	**280**	**320**	**240**	**460**

For the **machine hours** budget you'll need to know the quantities of

Product	Units produced	Hours per unit	Hours required
A	X	X	X
B	X	X	X
C	X	X	X
Total machine hours required			X
Factory machine hours available = number of machines x maximum hours for each			X
Additional machine hours required			X
			Quantity
Number of machines to hire (round this figure up) = additional hours / maximum hours per machine			X

Cash budgeting

A business will normally prepare monthly cash budgets that detail the anticipated cash inflows and outflows of the business. This allows the business to carry out appropriate financial planning for borrowing if required, and investment if a cash surplus is available. Information from all the other budgets will be needed to produce a meaningful cash budget'.

Cash inflows	Cash outflows
Revenue receipts • cash sales • receipts from credit customers **Capital receipts** • taking out a loan • issue of more shares • sale of non-current assets	**Revenue payments** • cash purchases • payments to credit suppliers • wage payments • payment of bills/expenses **Capital payments** • repayment of loans • purchase of non-current assets **Tax payments** • dividends/loan interest/ drawings

CBT focus

When preparing a cash budget, you will have to recognise the appropriate cash flows to be included, based on SFP and IS movements. However, in the exam you will be given a pro-forma for the cash budget, which will indicate which figures are relevant.

Cash flow forecast	£	£
Opening Cash balance / (Overdraft)		-65,500
Sales revenue		2,575,000
Expenditure		
Materials	1,710,500	
Labour	196,800	
Production overheads	40,420	
Other overheads	360,000	
Capital expenditure	120,000	2,427,720
Closing cash balance / (overdraft)		81,780

chapter

9

Further aspects of budgeting

- Preparing budgets with limiting factors.
- Cost classifications.
- Cost behaviour.
- Splitting semi-variable costs.
- Dealing with uncertainty.
- Flexing budgets.
- Flexible budgets.
- Feed forward control.

Preparing budgets with limiting factors

The level of activity at which a business can operate will very seldom be unlimited. Limitations may be imposed, for example, by:

- market demand for its products or services;
- the number of skilled employees available;
- the availability of material supplies;
- the space available either as a working area or for the storage of goods;
- the amount of cash or credit facilities available to finance the business.

Where one particular limitation is of major importance it may be necessary to budget for that item first and to construct the rest of the budget around it. the item concerned may be referred to as the principal budget factor or key factor.

Quite commonly, the rate of growth in sales is the principal budget factor and this would have to be forecast before any other budget plans were made.

It is essential to identify the principal budget factor and any other limiting factors at an early stage in the budgeting process so that management may consider whether:

- it is possible to overcome the limitation which they impose (e.g. by finding new markets for sales or by obtaining alternative supplies or substitute raw materials);
- the limitations imposed must be accepted and the business's budgets must be produced within those limitations.

As well as the limiting factor analysis that we saw in chapter 3, we may have to adjust our budget to reflect the limitations. This could be through buying and making more in one period, holding higher inventory to overcome limitations in future periods.

Or it may be that we require overtime, external assistance to overcome the limitations or we may just have to make less than we'd hoped.

Example 1:

A manufacturer makes a single product, this product is unique and requires 2.4kg of a very rare ingredient. Due to its rarity, there will only be 60,000kg available in the coming year.

The manufacturer is planning to make and sell 32,000 units in the coming year.

The number of units that can be produced in total is (60,000kg/2.4kg =) 25,000 units

There is a shortfall of 16,800 kg

This is equivalent to 7,000 units

Example 2:

A manufacturing business has made a budget that involves making and selling 50,000 units for the upcoming financial year.

Due to some specification changes and increased legislation the quality control department have highlighted a concern over their ability to meet the testing capacity to allow this to happen. They can test 3,600 units each month.

All units must be tested before they can be sold. They business hold no opening or closing inventory.

Units that require testing: 50,000

Units that can be tested internally (3,600 × 12 =) 43,200

Units to be tested by an alternative source: 6,800

Cost classifications

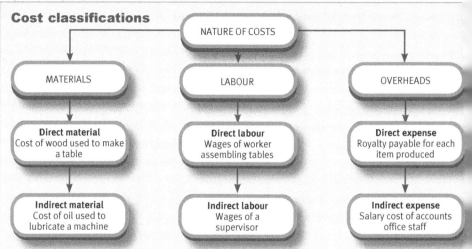

Indirect costs are also knows as overheads.

Production indirect costs are indirect costs involved in the production process, e.g. supervisor salary costs.

Non-production indirect costs are indirect costs involved in converting finished goods into revenue, e.g. administrative staff costs.

Cost behaviour

| A **variable cost** increases as the level of activity increases. | A **fixed cost** does not increase as the level of activity increases. |

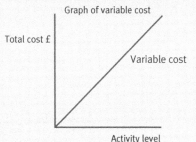

Graph of variable cost

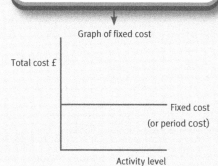

Graph of fixed cost

Examples of variable costs:

Direct materials

Direct labour

Examples of fixed costs:

Business rates

Management salaries

A **semi-variable cost** is one that contains both fixed and variable elements.

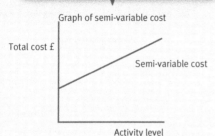

Graph of semi-variable cost

Total cost £

Semi-variable cost

Activity level

Semi-variable costs are also known as **semi-fixed costs** or **mixed costs**.

Examples of semi-variable costs:

Electricity costs – standing charge (fixed cost)
– cost per unit used (variable cost)

Salesman's salary – basic (fixed) + bonus (variable)

A **stepped cost** is one that remains fixed over a certain range of activity, but increases if activity increases beyond that level.

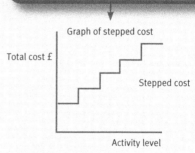

Graph of stepped cost

Total cost £

Stepped cost

Activity level

Examples of stepped costs:

Inventory storage costs

Supervisor salaries

Splitting semi-variable costs

High/low method

If a semi-variable cost is incurred, it is often necessary to estimate the fixed and variable elements of the cost for the purposes of budgeting. The costs can be split using the **High/low Method**.

$$\text{Variable cost per unit (VC)} = \frac{\text{Change in total cost}}{\text{Change in level of production}}$$

Fixed cost = Total cost – (VC x units produced)

Dealing with uncertainty

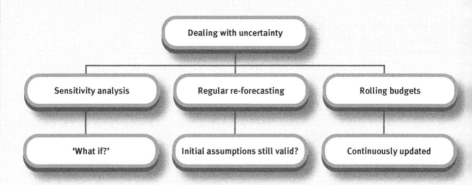

Flexing budgets

- For variances to be meaningful and appropriate for use as decision-making tools, a **flexed budget** should be prepared to take into account the change between the budgeted levels of activity (sales and production) and the actual levels.

	Budget	Flexed budget	Actual
Sales volume	100 units	90 units	90 units
Sales value	£1,000	£900	£990
Variable costs	£500	£450	£495
Fixed costs	£200	£200	£210
Profit	£300	£250	£285

Flexible budgets

A **fixed** budget contains information on costs and revenue for one level of activity. A **flexible** budget shows the same information, but for a number of different levels of activity.

	Low	Normal	High
Activity level	80,000 units	100,000 units	120,000 units
Revenue	£3,200,000	£4,000,000	£4,800,000
Variable costs	£1,440,000	£1,800,000	£2,160,000
Fixed costs	£300,000	£300,000	£300,000
Profit	£1,460,000	£1,900,000	£2,340,000

A **flexible** budget model makes it possible to quickly amend the line items in the event of some unforeseen complication. For example, should sales volume suddenly drop, affecting the amount of generated revenue, the flexible format makes it easy to quickly change the amounts associated with specific line items to reflect the new set of circumstances.

The ability to quickly adjust a flexible budget to take into account changes in output levels or shifts in income means that a business can move quickly to meet the new circumstances. By contrast, a fixed budget, that is based on a single set of projections and allows no room for adjustments without going through a complicated approval process, wastes valuable time and money that could be used more efficiently.

Feed forward control

- Feed-forward control is defined as the 'forecasting of differences between actual and planned outcomes and the implementation of actions before the event, to avoid such differences.'

- In simpler terms, feedforward control is where a problem is identified and corrective action taken, before the problem occurs.

- An example would be using a cash-flow budget to forecast a funding problem and as a result arranging a higher overdraft well in advance of the problem.

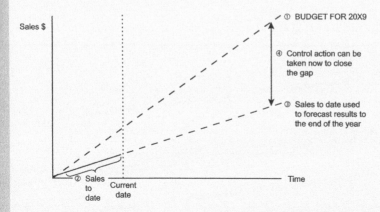

Advantages	Disadvantages
• It encourages managers to be pro active and deal with problems before they occur.	• It may be time consuming as control reports must be produced regularly.
• Re-forecasting on a monthly or continuous basis can save time when it comes to completing a quarterly or annual budget.	• It may require a sophisticated forecasting system, which might be expensive.

10

Standard costing and variances

- Standard costing.
- Variance analysis – overview.
- Sales variances.
- Material variances.
- Labour variances.
- Variable overhead variances.
- Fixed overhead variances.
- Variance investigation.

Key Point

Standard costing and variance analysis are very important topics.

Key themes include:

- Establishing a standard cost card – often needs to be done first to 'tidy up' the question.
- Calculating variances – show workings clearly.
- Explaining the causes of variances calculated. This is usually in the form of a memo so be careful about layout/format. Try to link variances to causes (look for clues in the task) and discuss whether they are controllable and whether they are likely to recur.

Standard costing

Objective is to control the business:

1. Set up standard costs, prepare budgets and set targets.

2. Measure actual performance.

3. Compare actual v budget via variances.

4. Investigate reasons for differences and take action.

Types of standard:

- Ideal standards are based on optimal operating conditions with maximum efficiency and are usually unobtainable under normal conditions.
- Attainable standards are based on efficient operating conditions.
- Basic standards are left unchanged from one period to another.
- Current standards are adjusted for each period.

Standard cost card

The standard cost card is a schedule that gives the standard costs that a unit of a product **should** incur.

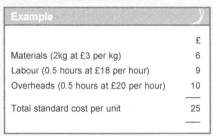

Example	
	£
Materials (2kg at £3 per kg)	6
Labour (0.5 hours at £18 per hour)	9
Overheads (0.5 hours at £20 per hour)	10
	—
Total standard cost per unit	25
	—

Advantages of standard costing

- Comparison of actual costs to standard enables management to judge performance.
- Facilitates 'management by exception' – i.e. concentrate on investigating the most significant variances.
- Simplifies bookkeeping if Inventories are valued at standard.

Disadvantages of standard costing

- Standards can quickly become out of date.
- Establishing standards, monitoring of system and investigation of variances is costly.
- Unrealistic standards can demotivate staff.

Variance analysis – overview

Comparing like with like

When calculating variances it is vital that you compare like with like.

For each cost we compare the actual cost with how much it **should** have cost to produce the same actual level of output:

Actual cost

↕ Variance

Standard cost of
actual production

Sales variances

Total sales variance

Sales price variance

Sales volume variance

Actual Quantity Sold x Actual Price — (AQ AP) ⎫
Actual Quantity Sold x Standard Price — (AQ SP) ⎬ Price Variance

Actual Quantity Sold x Standard Margin — (AQ SM) ⎫
Budget Quantity x Standard Margin — (BQ SM) ⎬ Volume Variance

Note: 'Margin' = contribution per unit (marginal costing) or profit per unit (absorption costing).

Materials variances

Materials Price variance

This is based on the actual quantity of materials purchased:

Materials purchased did cost

Actual quantity purchased $\times$ Actual price $= X$

Materials purchased should have cost

Actual quantity purchased $\times$ Standard price $= X$

} Price variance

Materials Usage variance

Quantity actually used at SP

Actual quantity used $\times$ Standard price $= X$

Quantity that should have been used at SP

Standard quantity used* $\times$ Standard price $= X$

} Usage variance

* i.e. quantity that should have been used to make actual output.

Reasons for variances

Price Variance

1. Wrong standards.
2. Lower/higher quality material.
3. Different supplier.
4. Good/poor purchasing.
5. External factors (inflation, exchange rates etc).

Usage Variance

1. Wrong standards.
2. Lower/higher quality of material.
3. Lower/higher quality of labour.
4. Theft.

Example

CBA focus

To determine whether the cost variances are favourable or adverse, you use common sense (e.g. if the actual price or quantity of materials used increased compared to standard, the variance is adverse).

Materials Variances

The standard cost of materials for each unit of production is

3kg @ £5/kg = £15 per unit

In May the firm bought 1,000kg of materials at a price of £5.10/kg. Of this 800kg was used to make 270 units of output.

Calculate the materials variances.

Solution:

Materials Price variance

Material purchased did cost	= 1,000 x 5.10	=	5,100	
Material purchased should have cost	= 1,000 x 5	=	5,000	100 (Adv.)

Materials Usage variance

Quantity atually used at SP	= 800 x 5	=	4,000	
Quantity that should have been used at SP	= 810* x 5	=	4,050	50 (Fav.)

*270 x 3 = 810kg

Example

A Ltd makes car parts. The budget and actual results for a part X for October 2008 were as follows.

	Budget	Actual
Production (units)	2,000	2,400
Direct materials	50kgs £6,000	45kgs £5,900

Calculate the following

(a) Standard price of materials per kilogram

(b) Standard usage of materials for actual production

(c) Direct materials price variance

(d) Direct materials usage variance

Solution

(a) Standard price of materials per kilogram
£6,000/50kg = £120 per kg

(b) Standard usage of materials for actual production

Standard usage for one unit = 50kg/2,000 = 0.025 kg

Standard usage for actual production = 0.025 x 2,400 = 60 kg

(c) Direct materials price variance

45 kg did cost	£5,900
45 kg should have cost 45 x £120	£5,400
Price variance	500(A)

(d) Direct materials usage variance

2,400 units did use 45 kg which should have cost at standard price 45 x £120	£5,400
2,400 units should have used 60kg which should have cost at standard price 60 x £120	£7,200
Usage variance	£1,800 (F)

Tutorial note

Total actual cost from data in question	£5,900
(£6,000/2,000 units) x 2,400 units =	
Total material budget cost of 2,400 units from data in question =	£7,200
Total variance	£1,300 (F)

Variances per answer:

Price	£500 (A)
Usage	£1,800 (F)
	£1,300 (F)

Labour variances

Labour Rate variance

Hours paid did cost

Actual hours $\times$ Actual rate $=$ X

Hours paid should have cost

Actual hours $\times$ Standard rate $=$ X

$\dfrac{\bullet}{\bullet}$ Rate variance

Labour Efficiency variance

Hours actually paid at SR

Actual hours $\times$ Standard rate $=$ X

Hours that should have been paid at SR

Standard hours* $\times$ Standard rate $=$ X

$\dfrac{\bullet}{\bullet}$ Efficiency variance

* i.e. hours firm should have worked to make the actual output

Reasons for variances

Rate Variance

1. Wrong standards.
2. Wage inflation.
3. Lower/higher skilled employees.
4. Unplanned overtime or bonuses.

Efficiency variance

1. Wrong standards.
2. Lower/higher morale.
3. Lower/higher skilled employees.
4. Lower/higher quality of material.

Example

Labour variances

The standard cost of labour for each unit
of production is

4hrs @ £10/hour = £40 per unit

In June the firm worked 2,500 hours, costing
£9.50 per hour, and made 600 units of output.
Calculate the labour variances.

Solution:

Labour Rate variance

Hours paid did cost	=	2,500 x 9.50	= 23,750	} 1,250 (F)
Hours paid should have cost	=	2,500 x10	= 25,000	

Labour Efficiency variance

Hours actually paid at SR	=	2,500 x 10	= 25,000	} 1,000 (A)
Hours that should have been paid at SR	=	2,400* x 10	= 24,000	

* 600 x 4 = 2,400hrs

Example

A Ltd makes car parts. The budget and actual results for a part X for October 2008 were as follows.

	Budget	Actual
Production (units)	2,000	2,400
Direct labour	500hrs £10,000	600hrs £11,000

Calculate the following

(a) Standard labour rate per hour

(b) Standard labour hours for actual production

(c) Direct labour rate variance

(d) Direct labour efficiency variance

Solution

(a) Standard labour rate per hour
    £10,000/500hr = £20 per hr

(b) Standard labour hours for actual production

Standard labour hours for one unit = 500/2,000 = 0.25 hrs

Standard labour hours for actual production = 0.25 x 2,400 = 600 hrs

(c) Direct labour rate variance

600 hrs did cost	£11,000
600 hrs should have cost 600x £20 =	£12,000
Labour rate variance	£1,000 (F)

(d) Direct labour efficiency variance

2,400 units did use 600 hrs which should have cost at standard rate 600 x £20	£12,000
2,400 units should have used 600hrs which should have cost at standard rate 600 x £20	£12,000
Labour efficiency variance	£nil

Tutorial note – reconciling the total variance

Total actual cost from data in question = (£10,000/500units) x 600 units =	£11,000
Total labour budget cost of 2,400 units from data in question	£12,000
Total variance	£1,000 (F)

Variances per answer:	
Labour rate	£1,000 (F)
Labour efficiency	nil
	£1,000 (F)

Idle Time Variance

If there is ide time, the rate variance is based on the hours actually paid whilst the efficiency variance is based on the hours actually worked.

Idles time variance:

Actual hours worked x standard rate per hour	x
Actual hours paid x standard per hour	(x)
Idle time variance	$\overline{(x)}$ (A)

Typical causes (idle time variance):

- **Industrial action** by the work force: 'Working to rule'.
- **Poor supervision**.
- Unexpected lost time due to **production bottlenecks** and resource shortages.

Variable overhead variances

Variable overhead expenditure variance
Hours worked did cost
Actual hours worked   x   Actual rate   = X
Hours worked should have cost
Actual hours worked   x   Standard rate   = X   Expenditure variance

Variable overhead efficiency variance
Hours actually worked at SR
Actual hours worked   x   Standard rate   = X
Hours that should have been worked at SR
Standard hours*   x   Standard rate   = X   Efficiency variance

* i.e. hours firm should have worked to make the actual output

Reasons for variances

Expenditure Variance

1. Wrong standards.
2. Rate inflation.

Efficiency variance

1. Wrong standards.
2. Lower/higher morale.
3. Lower/higher skilled employees.
4. Lower/higher quality of material.

Variable overhead variances

The standard cost of variable overhead for each unit of production is

  4hrs @ £3/hour = £12 per unit

In June the firm worked 2,500 hours, costing £3.20 per hour, and made 600 units of output. Calculate the variable overhead variances.

Solution:

Variable overhead expenditure variance

Hours worked did cost	= 2,500 x 3.20	= 8,000
Hours worked should have cost	= 2,500 x 3.00	= 7,500

500 (A)

Variable overhead efficiency variance

Hours worked should have cost	= 2,500 x 3.00	= 7,500
Hours that should have been worked at SR	= 2,400*x 3.00	= 7,200

300 (A)

* 600 x 4 = 2,400hrs

Tutorial note – reconciling the total variance

Total actual cost from data in question = 2,500 x £3.20 =	£8,000
Total budgeted cost of 2,400 units from data in question	£7,200
Total variance	£800 (A)

Variances per answer:

Variable overhead expenditure	£500 (A)
Variable overhead efficiency	£300 (A)
	£800 (A)

Fixed overhead variances

Definition

The total fixed overhead variance is the difference between:

the actual fixed overhead, and the absorbed fixed overhead.

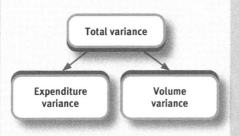

Fixed overhead expenditure variance (MC and TAC)

Actual fixed overheads $= X$

Budgeted fixed overheads $= X$

} Expenditure variance

Note: this is the original budget unadjusted for differences in output.

Fixed overhead volume variance (TAC only)

The volume variance is the difference between the budgeted overhead absorbed and the actual overhead absorbed.

Budgeted production $\times$ Standard cost per unit $= X$

Actual production $\times$ Standard cost per unit $= X$

} Volume var.

Reasons for fixed overhead variances

Fixed Overhead Expenditure Variance (MC and TAC)

The expenditure variance is the simplest fixed overhead variance and simply compares the original budgeted figure with actual. The variance will be due to poor budgeting or to a price rise.

e.g. rent increased by landlord.

Fixed Overhead Volume Variance (TAC)

The volume variance is due to the volume of production changing. A favourable (adverse) variance reflects the fact that more (less) units were made than planned. This could be due to:

- Poor budgeting
- Labour efficiency
- Availability of resources (e.g. shortage of materials).

Example

A Ltd makes car parts. The budget and actual results for a part X for October 2008 were as follows.

	Budget	Actual
Production (units)	2,000	2,400
Fixed overhead	£6,000	£7,000

Calculate the following

(a) Budgeted overhead absorption rate per unit

(b) Fixed overheads absorbed into actual production

(c) Fixed overhead expenditure variance

(d) Fixed overhead volume variance

Solution

(a) Budgeted overhead absorption rate per unit
£6,000/2,000 = £3 per unit

(b) Fixed overheads absorbed into actual production.

Units actually produced = 2,400 units

Overheads absorbed into actual production = 2,400 x £3 = £7,200

(c) Fixed overhead expenditure variance

Actual overhead	£7,000
Budgeted overhead	£6,000
	£1,000(A)

(d) Fixed overhead volume variance

Budgeted overhead =	£6,000
Actual overhead absorbed =	£7,200
Variance	£1,200 (F)

Tutorial note – reconciling the total variance

You are not asked to reconcile the fixed overhead variance, but you could do this as follows.

Actual overhead	7,000
Overhead absorbed	7,200
Total variance	£200 (F)

Variances per answer:	
Expenditure variance	£1,000 (A)
Volume variance	£1,200 (F)
	£200 (F)

Materials variances with inventory

If all materials purchased are not sold in the period, the inventory remaining is valued at standard cost not actual cost. This means that the price variance is calculated on all the inventory purchased, not just the inventory used.

<table>
<tr><td colspan="2">Example</td></tr>
</table>

A Ltd purchases 1,000 kg of materials at a cost of £2,100. It uses 900 kg of materials to make 500 products. The standard cost card for materials is:

	Standard cost per unit £
Materials – 2 kg at £2 per kg =	4

Calculate the price variance, usage variance and the value of closing inventory.

Solution

(a) **Price variance**

1,000 kg did cost	£2,100
1,000 kg should cost 1,000 x £2 =	£2,000
Price variance	£100 (A)

(b) **Usage variance**

500 products did use 900 kg at £2 =	£1,800
500 products should use 1,000 kg at £2 =	£2,000
Usage variance	£200 (F)

(c) **Value of closing inventory**

100kg x £2 =	£200

CBA focus

As well as calculating variances and explaining their possible causes, you may have to discuss whether or not they should be investigated.

In addition the examiners have indicated that calculations could take the following form:

- You may be given variances and asked to work backwards.
- You may have to split the variance to identify the impact of inflation.

Variance investigation

Variance calculations are just the starting point. Next, management need to decide which variances are worth investigating. To do this they will consider the following.

- How big is the variance?
  - Absolute size.
  - Relative size as a % of standard.
  - Overall trend.
- Is it favourable or adverse?
- Possible reasons for it.
  - Planning errors.
  - Measurement problems.
  - Random factors.
  - Operational issues.
- Controllability.
- Cost v benefit of investigation.
- Likelihood of a problem, based on past experience.
- The overall picture given by all the variances.

Management will seek to assign responsibility for the variances so they can be investigated further.

Performance measurement and control

- Types of performance indicator.
- Introduction.
- Ratio analysis.
- Profitability ratios.
- Working capital ratios.
- Additional ratios.
- The balanced scorecard.
- Ethics.

Types of performance indicator

Performance appraisal is a very important topic. Two styles of task are commonplace:

Some tasks ask you to assess the organisation using ratios and other KPIs.

Some tasks give some new circumstances and require you to produce forecasts/revised ratios based on those changes.

Try to relate your comments to any details given in the scenario:

e.g. a switch to more expensive materials could explain changes in margins and quality.

Try to discuss both financial and non-financial indicators.

Introduction

An effective system of performance measurement is critical if the business is to be controlled.

Performance indicators can be:

- quantitative (i.e. expressed in numbers); or

- qualitative (i.e. not expressed in numbers). For example, satisfied/not satisfied or grade poor to excellent.

Ratio analysis

Benchmarking

Need a suitable basis for comparison.

- Internal benchmarking. For example, by division.
- Competitive benchmarking.
- Activity (or process) benchmarking.
- Generic benchmarking – look at conceptually similar processes.

Profitability ratios

Return on capital employed (ROCE)

The AAT have stipulated that net assets should be used for capital employed. Net assets is total equity or can be calculated as total assets – total liabilities. Return on capital employed is frequently regarded as the best measure of profitability.

$$ROCE = \frac{\text{Profit before interest and taxation (PBIT)}}{\text{Capital employed}} \times 100\%$$

Note that the profit before interest is used, because the loan capital rewarded by that interest is included in capital employed.

A low return on capital employed (assets used) is caused by either a low profit margin or a low asset turnover or both. This can be seen by breaking down the primary ROCE ratio into its two components: profit margin and asset turnover.

$$ROCE = \frac{PBIT}{Capital\ employed}$$
$$= \frac{PBIT}{Revenue} \times \frac{Revenue}{Capital\ employed}$$
$$= Profit\ margin \times Asset\ turnover$$

Profit margin (on revenue)

$$Profit\ margin = \frac{Profit\ before\ interest\ and\ taxation}{Revenue} \times 100\%$$

A low margin indicates low selling prices or high costs or both.

Asset turnover

This will show the extent to which a company is utilising its assets to generate turnover:

$$Asset\ turnover = \frac{Revenue}{Capital\ employed}$$

A low turnover shows that a company is not generating a sufficient volume of business for the size of the asset base. This may be remedied by increasing sales or by disposing of some of the assets or both.

Gross profit margin

$$Gross\ profit\ margin = \frac{Gross\ profit}{Revenue} \times 100\%$$

The gross profit margin focuses on the trading account. A low margin could indicate selling prices too low or cost of sales too high.

Working capital ratios

Receivables collection period (Receivable days)

This is computed by dividing the receivables by the average daily sales to determine the number of days' sales held in receivables.

$$\text{Receivables collection period} = \frac{\text{Trade receivables}}{\text{Credit sales}} \times 365 \text{ days}$$

A long average collection period probably indicates poor credit control. If a company offers standard terms to its credit customers (e.g. 30 days credit), then the actual period of credit taken can be compared to the standard period.

Payables payment period

This is computed by dividing the payables by the average daily credit purchases to determine the number of days purchases held in payables. This tells us how long we are taking to pay our creditors. Too long a payment period may mean that they refuse to sell us goods in the future.

$$\text{Payables payment period} = \frac{\text{Trade payables}}{\text{Credit purchases}} \times 365 \text{ days}$$

Inventory holding period

This ratio indicates whether inventory levels are justified in relation to sales.

$$\text{Inventory holding period} = \frac{\text{Inventory}}{\text{Cost of sales}} \times 365 \text{ days}$$

Working capital cycle = receivables period + inventory period – payables period.

Additional ratios

In the assessment candidates could be asked to calculate other useful/sensible indicators depending on the business and the information provided.

For example: if the theme of the task was a training college, they may give the number of students who took the course and the number of students who passed the exam first time.

From this a useful performance indicator would be:

$$\% \text{ students that pass first time} = \frac{\text{number of students who passed the exam first time}}{\text{number of students who took the course}} \times 100$$

Flexibility, understanding and common sense are vital in this type of task.

Adding value

Added value = sales price – cost of bought-in goods and services.

Others, depending on the scenario:

Output per employee.

Sales per employee.

Number of defects.

Delivery time to customer.

Rooms cleaned per hour.

The balanced scorecard

From strategic objectives to performance indicators

The balanced scorecard performance management system

	Financial perspective	**Customer perspective**	**Internal business process perspective**	**Innovation and learning perspective**
Strategic objective	Shareholder satisfaction	Customer satisfaction	Manufacturing excellence	New product innovation
CSF	Grow shareholder wealth	Achieve preferred supplier status	State-of-the-art process plant	Successful new product development
KPIs	• ROCE • Growth %	• Number of customer partnerships	• Cycle times • Unit cost • % yield	• % of revenues represented by new products

Ethics

Definition

Ethics is the analysis of right and wrong an associated responsibility.

AAT's code of professional ethics

- Integrity
- Objectivity
- Professional care and due competence
- Confidentiality
- Professional behaviour

The main focus will be on practical business ethics relating to product design and the life cycle of a product, value analysis considerations and goal congruence issues given the performance indicators of a company.

Example

Giving a manager a target and rewarding a bonus relating to profit may cause the manger to behave unethically as their objectivity may be compromised. They may make unnecessary cost cuts, for example making staff redundant. They may well hit their profit target but the long term success of the business could be hindered by the lost expertise from the staff leaving.

chapter 12

Divisional Performance

- Responsibility centres.
- Return on investment (ROI).
- Residual income.
- Transfer pricing.

Responsibility centres

Type of division	Description	Typical measures
Cost centre	• Division incurs costs but has no revenue stream.	• Total cost and cost per unit. • Cost variances. • NFPIs related to quality, productivity and efficiency.
Profit Centre	• Division has costs and revenue. • Manager **does not** have the authority to alter the level of investment in the division.	All of the above PLUS • Total sales and market share. • Profit. • Sales variances. • Working capital ratios (depending on the division concerned). • NFPIs e.g. related to productivity, quality and customer satisfaction.
Investment centre	• Division has costs and revenue. • Manager **does** have the authority to invest in new assets or dispose of existing ones.	All of the above PLUS • ROI. • RI.

Return on Investment (ROI)

An understanding of the drawbacks of ROI is essential for the exam.

$$ROI = \frac{\text{Pre tax controllable profit}}{\text{Controllable capital employed}}$$

Advantages of ROI	Disadvantages of ROI
• Relative measure (%), therefore aids comparisons between divisions of different sizes.	• May lead to dysfunctional decision making e.g. a division with a current ROI of 30% would not wish to accept a project offering an ROI of 25% as this would dilute its current figure.
• Used externally (ROCE) and therefore understood by users.	
• Encourages good use of existing capital resources.	• ROI increases as assets get older if NBVs are used, thus giving managers an incentive to hang on to possibly inefficient obsolete machines.
• It can be broken down into secondary ratios for more detailed analysis.	• It may encourage the manipulation of profit and capital employed.
	• Different accounting policies can confuse comparisons.

Residual Income (RI)

RI = Pre tax controllable profits – imputed charge for controllable invested capital

Advantages of RI	Disadvantages of RI
• Reduces the problem of rejecting projects with ROIs greater than the group target but less than the division's current ROI.	• Does not facilitate comparisons between divisions of different sizes.
• Cost of financing a division is brought home to divisional managers.	• Profit and capital employed may be subject to manipulation.

Transfer pricing

Objectives

- Goal congruence – divisional decisions are the correct decisions for the group.
- Performance measurement.
- Autonomy.
- Minimising global tax liability.
- To record the movement of goods and services.

Exam questions

Will often be given a TP and asked to comment. Look at the following.

- Implications for divisional performance – e.g. is a target ROI achieved?
- Resulting manager behaviour – does it give dysfunctional decision making – e.g. will a manager reject a new product that is acceptable to the company as a whole?

Rules

- In a perfectly competitive market, TP = market price.
- If spare capacity exists, TP = marginal cost.
- With production constraints, TP = marginal cost + opportunity cost of not using those resources elsewhere.

Practical transfer pricing systems

Market price

- Will be seen as fair by managers.
- Does an external market exist for the component?
- Prices may be linked to volume, so which to use?
- May be more than one market price – which to use?
- Are costs of selling externally the same as for internal transfers?

Production cost + mark-up

- Marginal or full cost?
- Full cost can cause problems as TP viewed as a variable cost by the receiving division.
- Standard cost aids responsibility accounting.

Negotiation

- Look at bargaining power of different parties.

Two-part transfer

- The price is charged in 2 instalments.
- The first is standard marginal cost.
- The second is a lump sum figure at the end of the period to give the supplying division profit incentive.

Dual pricing

- The receiving division records the transfer at the best price from their perspective, usually standard marginal cost.

- The supplying division records the transfer at the best price from their perspective, usually market price.
- Both divisions feel they are being appraised on a fair basis, but there are internal adjustments required.

13

Long term decision making

- Payback period.
- ARR.
- Time value of money and discounting.
- Net present value (NPV).
- Internal rate of return (IRR).
- Calculation of the IRR.

Payback period

Definition

Payback period: the amount of time it takes for an investment project to recover the cash cost of the original investment.

CBA focus

Assume cash accrues evenly throughout the year unless told otherwise.

Example

A machine is purchased for £150,000 and is expected to have a useful life of five years. Estimated cash savings over the useful life of the machine are as follows:

Year	£
1	40,000
2	75,000
3	60,000
4	30,000
5	30,000

The payback period for this investment is:

Year	Cash flow	Cumulative cash flow
0	−150,000	−150,000
1	40,000	−110,000
2	75,000	−35,000
3	60,000	25,000

Payback occurs after 2 years and 7 months

Months are calculated 35/60 × 12 = 7

Advantages and disadvantages of payback period

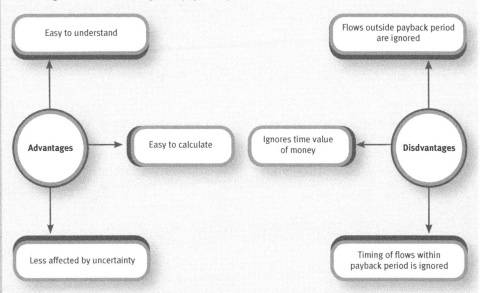

Advantages

Easy to understand

Easy to calculate

Less affected by uncertainty

Disdvantages

Flows outside payback period are ignored

Ignores time value of money

Timing of flows within payback period is ignored

ARR

There are two possible ways to calculate the ARR. One uses the initial capital costs:

$$ARR = \frac{\text{average annual profits before interest and tax}}{\text{initial capital costs}} \times 100$$

The alternative approach is to use the average value of the cpital invested:

$$ARR = \frac{\text{average annual profits before interest and tax}}{\text{average capital investment}} \times 100$$

The average investment can be calculated ir a similar way to most averages by adding the investment cash flows together and dividing by the number of flows. This is usually an initial invest ment value plus a residual value at the end of the investment, often referred to as scrap value.

$$\text{Average capital investment} = \frac{\text{initial investment} + \text{scrap value}}{2}$$

These formulas are not given in the exam and must be learnt.

Time value of money and discounting

Key Point

A key concept in long-term decision-making is that money has a time value.

Key Point

Only 'relevant' cash flows should be included when assessing a decision.

Definition

Present value (PV): The value at today's date of an amount of cash received/paid at some time in the future, taking account of the compound interest earned over the relevant period.

Definition

Relevant cash flows: Future incremental cash flows that arise if a decision is adopted.

Present value = Future cash flow x Discount factor

Net present value (NPV)

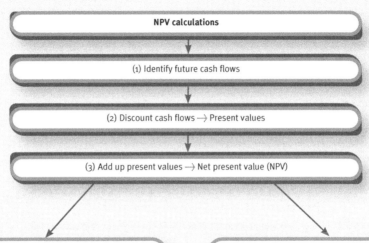

NPV calculations

↓

(1) Identify future cash flows

↓

(2) Discount cash flows ---→ Present values

↓

(3) Add up present values ---→ Net present value (NPV)

NPV = Positive
- Accept project
- PV Cash inflows > PV Cash outflows

NPV = Negative
- Reject project
- PV Cash outflows > PV Cash inflows

Example

Rug Limited is considering a capital investment in new equipment with estimated cash flows as follows:

Year	0	1	2	3	4	5
Cash flow (£)	(240,000)	80,000	120,000	70,000	40,000	20,000

The company's cost of capital is 9%.

Year	Cash flow £	Discount factor	Present value £
0	(240,000)	1.000	(240,000)
1	80,000	0.917	73,360
2	120,000	0.842	101,040
3	70,000	0.772	54,040
4	40,000	0.708	28,320
5	20,000	0.650	13,000
		Net present value =	29,760

Positive ∴ Accept

Internal rate of return (IRR)

Definition

IRR: the breakeven cost of capital for one investment opportunity. It is the interest rate or discount factor that means that the investment makes no profit or loss i.e. the NPV of the investment = 0

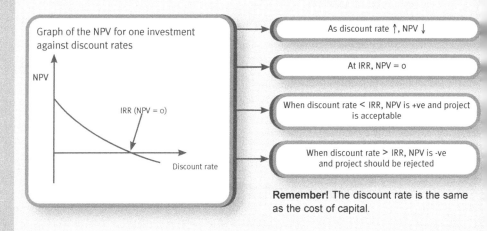

Graph of the NPV for one investment against discount rates

NPV

IRR (NPV = o)

Discount rate

As discount rate ↑, NPV ↓

At IRR, NPV = o

When discount rate < IRR, NPV is +ve and project is acceptable

When discount rate > IRR, NPV is -ve and project should be rejected

Remember! The discount rate is the same as the cost of capital.

Calculation of the IRR

By approximation

The approximate IRR of a project can be estimated by considering how close the NPVs of a project are to zero.

The method used to estimate the IRR is as follows:

- Calculate two NPVs for the investment at different discount rates.
- Estimate the IRR with reference to the NPV values.

If a project has an NPV of £4,400 at 10% and -£31,000 at 20% it can be estimated that the IRR will be closer to 10% than 20% as £4,400 is closer to zero than -£31,000. The IRR will be approximately 11%

By calculation

The IRR of an investment can also be calculated using linear interpolation i.e. it uses two known points on a graph and joins them with a straight line. The point where the line crosses the x-axis will be calculated to provide the IRR.

The method used to calculate the IRR is as follows:

- Calculate two NPVs for the investment at different discount rates
- Use the following formula to find the IRR:

$$IRR (\%) = L + \frac{NL}{(NL - NH)} \times (H - L)$$

Where:

L = Lower rate of interest

H = Higher rate of interest

NL = NPV at lower rate of interest

NH = NPV at higher rate of interest

Using the values above:

$$IRR\ (\%) = 10 + \frac{4,400}{(4,400 - 31,000)} \times (20 - 10)$$

$$IRR\ (\%) = 10 + \frac{4,400}{35,400} \times 10$$

$$IRR\ (\%) = 11.24\%$$

14

Impact of Technology

- Technological advancements.
- Cloud computing.
- Data analytics.
- Big data.
- Artificial intelligence and machine learning.
- Data visualisation.

Technological advancements

Benefits of technological advancements

- Speed
- Automation
- Efficiency
- Focus

Challenges faced by organisations adopting technological advancements

- Change management
- Skills and expertise
- Integration issues
- Legislation
- Cost benefit
- Cyber security
- Staying up to date

Cloud computing

Cloud computing is defined as the **delivery of on-demand computing resources**. Users log into an account in order to access, manage and process files and software via remote servers hosted on the internet. The cloud setup can be **public** or **private**.

Cloud accounting is using cloud computing to run accounting software and programs.

Advantages

- Flexibility and scalability
- Cost efficient
- Security
- Flexible working
- Environment

Disadvantages

- Organisational change
- Contract management
- Security, privacy and reliance
- Contract management

Data analytics

Data analytics is the process of collecting, organising and analysing large sets of data (big data) to discover patterns and other information which the organisation can use to inform future decisions.

Benefits (McKinsey):

- Fresh insight and understanding
- Performance improvement
- Improved segmentation and customisation
- Better decision making
- Innovation
- Risk management

Big data

Big data describes data sets (structured and unstructured) so large and varied they are beyond the capability of traditional data-processing.

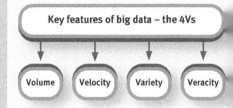

Artificial intelligence and machine learning

Artificial intelligence (AI) is an area of computer science that emphasises the creation of intelligent machines that work and react like human beings.

Machine learning is a subset of AI, in which AI computer code is built to effectively mimic how the human brain works.

Activities and skills AI can master include:

- Voice recognition
- Planning
- Learning
- Problem solving

Process automation

The technology enabled automation of complex business processes. This can be entire processes or elements therein aimed at improving consistency, quality, speed, whilst delivering cost savings.

Some of the technological developments described in this chapter enable advanced process automation, now capable of making decisions using reasoning, language and learned behaviour.

Professions most at risk from automation include data entry, tax preparation, insurance underwriters, mathematical technicians, telemarketers and accounts clerks.

Professions least at risk from automation include social workers, healthcare assistants, audiologists, occupational therapists, recreational therapists and mental health professionals.

Data visualisation

Allows large volumes of complex data to be displayed in a visually appealing and accessible way that facilitates the understanding and use of the underlying data.

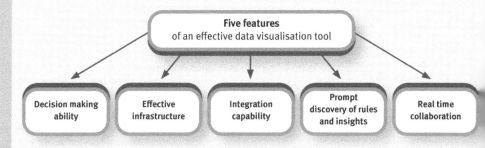

Index